30 MINUTES OR LESS | Favorite Foods

30 MINUTES OR LESS | Favorite Foods

p

This is a Parragon Publishing Book

First published in 2006

Parragon Publishing

Queen Street House

4 Queen Street

Bath BA1 1HE, UK

Copyright © Parragon Books Ltd 2006

ISBN: 1-40547-306-1

Printed in China

Produced by the Bridgewater Book Company Ltd.

Front cover photography by Mike Cooper

Front cover home economy by Sumi Glass

Notes for the Reader

This book uses imperial, metric, and US cup measurements. Follow the same units of measurement

throughout; do not mix imperial and metric. All spoon measurements are level: teaspoons are

assumed to be 5 ml, and tablespoons are assumed to be 15 ml. Unless otherwise stated,

milk is assumed to be whole milk, eggs and individual vegetables are medium, and pepper

is freshly ground black pepper.

Recipes using raw or very lightly cooked eggs should be avoided by infants, the elderly,

pregnant women, convalescents, and anyone suffering from an illness. Pregnant women and

breast-feeding women are advised to avoid eating peanuts and peanut products.

Contents

Introduction

Anyone who regularly cooks for themselves, family, or friends will have asked the question "What am I going to cook tonight?" The hard part is coming up with recipe ideas in the first place, and even your favorite meal can lose its appeal when it's in constant rotation.

EASE AND INSPIRATION

Written for everyone who loves food, these easy recipes have been specially chosen so that even the busiest people can cook their favorite food at home, and quickly, too. The book is organized into four recipe chapters: appetizers and snacks, main courses, accompaniments and light meals, and desserts. These offer tasty and imaginative suggestions for satisfying family suppers as well as stylish dinner parties, all requiring the minimum of time and effort. Recipes include favorite foods from around the world, from Asia to Mexico, with many well-loved stops along the way. There are traditional favorites, from Croque Monsieur and Garlic Bread to Pepper Steak and Caesar Salad, but you'll also find that many of these have been given a contemporary twist, being low in saturated fats and low in sugars for healthy and enjoyable eating.

All the recipes in this book can be completed in 30 minutes or less. There are no complicated cooking methods or elaborate presentations, nor will you need to use every pot and pan in the kitchen. Simple step-by-step directions and full-color photographs enable even the most inexperienced to cook with confidence and success.

If you're tired of serving up the same old meals day in, day out, bored with staring at the contents of your refrigerator, seeking inspiration, and you simply long for favorite recipes that are quick, healthy, and hassle-free, then look no farther. These flavor-packed meals will satisfy your appetite as well as your taste buds and renew your enthusiasm for cooking. They are achievable for anyone with a good knife and a few well-chosen pots and pans, so you'll never have an excuse for being in a culinary rut again.

TOP TIPS FOR TIME MANAGEMENT

Follow these handy hints to be sure of making the most of the time you spend in the kitchen.

PLANNING

This is absolutely essential if you want to be efficient.

‣ Plan a week's menu and compile your shopping list from your recipes.

‣ Consider what's going on during the week—if you'll be out all day, forget doing a complicated meal like lasagna.

‣ Cook for the freezer—particularly with items like homemade tomato sauce for Italian dishes.

‣ Plan to have leftovers—a roast chicken one day can mean a stir-fry or soup on another day.

‣ Keep a good stock in your pantry and refrigerator of basic but versatile staples that can be dressed up or down as the need or your mood requires—rice, pasta, canned tomatoes, frozen meat and fish, frozen vegetables, and cheese are a good place to start.

‣ Don't wait until something runs out before you replace it— whenever you find something is three-quarters empty, put it on your shopping list and buy more (keep a notebook on the front of the refrigerator, if it helps).

‣ Read through the recipe before starting so that you can assemble your ingredients and all the kitchen equipment you'll need.

SORT, PURGE, AND ARRANGE

Clear counters and clean out drawers, shelves, and cupboards. Throw out or give away anything you don't use. Position the most frequently used items nearest the work area where they will be utilized, along with the other items they work with—this will prevent you from wasting time and energy traipsing back and forth across the kitchen and it will make your cooking activities more efficient.

Don't forget to clean up as you go along. Many people avoid cooking primarily because they simply cannot face the thought of the mess left at the end of the process. But if you put dirty utensils in the dishwasher or sink along the way, soak pans when necessary, and mop up spills when they occur, the entire kitchen experience becomes more enjoyable and less time-consuming.

Chapter One
Appetizers and Snacks

Croque Monsieur
25 minutes to the table

MAKES 2

ingredients

generous ¾ cup grated Gruyère or
   Emmental cheese
4 slices white bread, crusts removed
2 thick slices lean ham
1 small egg
about 3 tbsp unsalted butter

CHEESE SAUCE
2 tbsp unsalted butter
1 tsp sunflower-seed or corn oil
½ tbsp all-purpose flour
½ cup warm milk
¼ cup grated Gruyère or Emmental
   cheese
pepper

method

Spread half the grated cheese on 2 slices of the bread, then top each with a slice of ham, cut to fit. Sprinkle the ham with the remaining cheese, then top with the remaining slices of bread and press down.

To make the cheese sauce, melt the butter with the oil in a small, heavy-bottomed pan over medium heat. Stir in the flour, until well combined and smooth. Cook, stirring constantly, for 1 minute. Remove from the heat and stir in a little of the milk until well incorporated. Return to the heat and gradually add the remaining milk, stirring constantly. Cook, stirring, for another 3 minutes, or until the sauce is smooth and thickened. Remove from the heat and stir in the cheese, and pepper to taste, then set aside and keep warm.

Beat the egg in a soup dish or other flat bowl. Add 1 sandwich and press down to coat on both sides, then remove from the bowl and repeat with the other sandwich.

Preheat the broiler to high. Line a baking sheet with foil and set aside. Melt the butter in a skillet over medium-high heat. Add 1 or both sandwiches, depending on the size of your pan, and cook until golden brown on both sides. Add a little extra butter, if necessary, if you have to cook the sandwiches separately.

Transfer the sandwiches to the foil-lined baking sheet and spread the cheese sauce over the top. Cook under the broiler, about 4 inches/ 10 cm from the heat, for 4 minutes, or until golden and brown. Cut each sandwich in half diagonally and serve immediately.

Eggs Benedict with Quick Hollandaise Sauce

15 minutes to the table

SERVES 4

ingredients

1 tbsp white wine vinegar

4 eggs

2 English muffins

4 slices lean ham

QUICK HOLLANDAISE SAUCE

3 egg yolks

scant 1 cup butter

1 tbsp lemon juice

pepper

method

Fill a wide skillet three-quarters full with water and bring to a boil over low heat. Reduce the heat to a simmer and add the vinegar. When the water is barely simmering, carefully break the eggs into the skillet. Let cook for 1 minute, then, using a large spoon, gently loosen the eggs from the bottom of the skillet. Let cook for another 3 minutes, or until the white is cooked and the yolk is still soft, basting the top of the egg with the water from time to time.

Meanwhile, to make the hollandaise sauce, put the egg yolks in a food processor or blender. Melt the butter in a small pan until bubbling. Gradually add the hot butter in a steady stream through the feeder tube of the food processor or blender until the sauce is thick and creamy. Add the lemon juice, and a little warm water if the sauce is too thick, then season to taste with pepper. Remove from the food processor or blender and keep warm.

Split the English muffins and toast them on both sides. To serve, top each muffin with a slice of ham, a poached egg, and a generous spoonful of the hollandaise sauce.

caution

Recipes using raw eggs should be avoided by infants, the elderly, pregnant women, convalescents, and anyone suffering from an illness.

Brunch Bruschetta
10 minutes to the table

method

Toast the ciabatta bread.

Mix the tomato, scallions, mozzarella cheese, avocado, balsamic vinegar, and half the oil together in a bowl. Season to taste with salt and pepper.

Drizzle the remaining oil over the ciabatta toast and top with the tomato mixture.

Garnish with the basil and serve immediately.

SERVES 2

ingredients

4 slices ciabatta bread

1 large ripe tomato, diced

2 scallions, finely sliced

1 small fresh buffalo mozzarella cheese, diced

½ ripe avocado, skinned, pitted, and diced

½ tbsp balsamic vinegar

2 tbsp extra-virgin olive oil

salt and pepper

2 tbsp shredded fresh basil leaves, to garnish

Chickpea Dip
10 minutes to the table

SERVES 8

ingredients
1 lb/450 g canned chickpeas
juice of 2 large lemons
$\frac{2}{3}$ cup sesame seed paste
2 garlic cloves, crushed
4 tbsp extra-virgin olive oil
small pinch of ground cumin
salt and pepper

TO GARNISH
1 tsp paprika
chopped fresh flat-leaf parsley

TO SERVE
warm pitas
green olives (optional)

method
Drain the chickpeas, reserving a little of the can liquid, and put in a food processor or blender. Process until smooth, gradually adding the lemon juice and enough of the reserved liquid to form a smooth, thick puree. Add the sesame seed paste, garlic, 3 tablespoons of the oil, and the cumin, and process again until smooth. Season to taste with salt and pepper.

Turn the mixture into a shallow serving dish, then cover with plastic wrap and chill in the refrigerator until ready to serve.

To serve, mix the remaining oil with the paprika and drizzle over the top of the dip. Sprinkle with chopped parsley and accompany with warm pitas, and olives if using.

Broccoli and Cheese Soup

30 minutes to the table

method

Heat the butter in a large pot over medium heat. Add the onions and cook, stirring frequently, for 5-8 minutes, or until softened. Stir in the potato, then add the hot stock and bring to a boil. Reduce the heat and simmer for 5 minutes.

Add the broccoli and cook, stirring occasionally, for another 5 minutes. Season to taste with pepper. Transfer the soup to a food processor or blender, in batches, and process until smooth. Return to a clean pot.

Add the cream and cheese to the soup and cook over low heat, stirring, until the cheese has melted.

To serve, mash the remaining cheese with the remaining cream in a bowl.

Serve the soup hot in individual warmed bowls, along with the reserved cream and cheese, sprinkled with a few chives.

variation

To make bleu cheese croutons to serve with the soup, brush slices of a baguette with olive oil and toast in a low oven, until golden. Mash the cheese with only 1 tablespoon of heavy cream and spread onto the toasted bread. Float a crouton in each bowl of soup.

SERVES 4

ingredients

4 tbsp butter

2 onions, chopped

1 potato, peeled and diced

4 cups hot vegetable or chicken stock

1 head broccoli, broken into small florets

$\frac{2}{3}$ cup heavy cream, plus 3 tbsp to serve

2 cups crumbled bleu cheese, $\frac{1}{2}$ cup reserved to serve

pepper

$\frac{1}{4}$ oz/10 g fresh chives, snipped, to garnish

Gazpacho
15 minutes to the table

SERVES 4

ingredients

2 lb 4 oz/1 kg ripe tomatoes, skinned,
   seeded, and coarsely chopped
½ cucumber, skinned, seeded, and
   coarsely chopped
1 green bell pepper, seeded and
   coarsely chopped
4 oz/115 g fresh bread, crusts
   removed
1 small onion, coarsely chopped
1 garlic clove, chopped
1 tbsp white wine vinegar
½ cup olive oil
salt

TO GARNISH
small amount of tomatoes, cucumber,
   and green bell pepper mixture
a few sprigs of fresh basil

TO SERVE
ice cubes
fresh crusty bread

method

Set aside some of the tomatoes, cucumber, and green bell pepper for a garnish. Put the bread into a food processor and process until crumbs form. Add the remaining tomatoes, cucumber, and green bell pepper, along with the onion, garlic, vinegar, and oil, and process until smooth.

The tomatoes should have enough juice in them to make enough liquid, but add a little water if the soup is too thick. Season to taste with salt.

Divide the soup between 4 serving bowls and add a few ice cubes to make sure that the soup is served chilled. Garnish with the reserved tomatoes, cucumber, and green bell pepper. Add a few basil sprigs and serve with fresh crusty bread.

Pan-Fried Scallops and Shrimp

20 minutes to the table

SERVES 4

ingredients

12 shucked, cleaned raw scallops,
    thawed if frozen (see cook's tip)
12 raw large shrimp, shelled
    and deveined
2 tbsp all-purpose flour
3 tbsp olive oil
2 garlic cloves, finely chopped
2 tbsp chopped fresh parsley
3 tbsp lemon juice
salt and pepper

method

Using a sharp knife, cut the scallops in half, then season the scallops and shrimp to taste with salt and pepper. Spread the flour out on a plate. Coat the scallops and shrimp in the flour, shaking off any excess.

Heat the oil in a large, heavy-bottomed skillet over medium heat. Add the scallops and shrimp and cook, turning once, for 2 minutes. Add the garlic and parsley, then stir well, tossing the shellfish to coat, and cook, shaking the skillet occasionally, for 2 minutes, or until the scallops are opaque and the shrimp have turned pink.

Add the lemon juice and toss well to coat. Transfer to warmed plates and serve immediately.

cook's tip

If using frozen scallops, thaw out slowly in the refrigerator. Once they are completely thawed out, use immediately, or keep in the refrigerator until ready to cook but use on the same day.

Baked Eggs with Spinach
30 minutes to the table

method

Preheat the oven to 400°F/200°C.

Heat the oil in a skillet over medium heat. Add the shallots and cook, stirring frequently, for 4-5 minutes, or until softened. Add the spinach, then cover and cook for 2-3 minutes, or until the spinach has just wilted. Remove the lid and cook until all the liquid has evaporated.

Add the cream to the spinach mixture and season to taste with nutmeg and pepper. Spread the spinach mixture over the bottom of a shallow gratin pan, then make 4 wells in the mixture with the back of a spoon.

Crack an egg into each well and scatter over the Parmesan cheese. Bake in the preheated oven for 12-15 minutes, or until the eggs are set. Serve with toasted whole-wheat bread.

SERVES 4

ingredients

1 tbsp olive oil

3 shallots, finely chopped

1 lb 2 oz/500 g baby spinach leaves

4 tbsp light cream

freshly grated nutmeg

4 large eggs

4 tbsp finely grated Parmesan cheese

pepper

toasted whole-wheat bread, to serve

Prosciutto with Figs

10 minutes to the table

SERVES 4

ingredients

6 oz/175 g prosciutto, thinly sliced
4 fresh ripe figs
1 lime
2 sprigs fresh basil
pepper

method

Using a sharp knife, trim the visible fat from the slices of ham and discard. Arrange the ham on 4 large serving plates, loosely folding it so that it falls into decorative shapes. Season to taste with pepper.

Using a sharp knife, cut each fig lengthwise into 4 wedges. Arrange a fig on each serving plate. Cut the lime into 6 wedges, then put a wedge on each plate and reserve the remaining wedges. Remove the leaves from the basil sprigs and divide between the plates. Cover with plastic wrap and chill in the refrigerator, until ready to serve.

Just before serving, remove the plates from the refrigerator and squeeze the juice from the remaining lime wedges over the ham.

variations

This dish is also delicious made with 4 slices of Charentais melon or 12–16 cooked and cooled asparagus spears instead of the figs.

Nachos
20 minutes to the table

method

Preheat the oven to 400°F/200°C.

Spread the tortilla chips out over the bottom of a large, shallow ovenproof pan or roasting pan. Cover with the refried beans. Sprinkle over the chiles and pimientos and season to taste with salt and pepper. Mix the grated cheeses together in a bowl and sprinkle on top.

Bake in the preheated oven for 5–8 minutes, or until the cheese is bubbling and melted.

Serve immediately with guacamole and sour cream.

SERVES 6

ingredients

6 oz/175 g tortilla chips

14 oz/400 g canned refried beans, warmed

2 tbsp finely chopped bottled jalapeño chiles

7 oz/200 g canned or bottled pimientos or roasted bell peppers, drained and finely sliced

generous 1 cup grated Gruyère cheese

generous 1 cup grated Cheddar cheese

salt and pepper

TO SERVE

guacamole

sour cream

Scrambled Eggs with Asparagus
15 minutes to the table

method

Melt half the butter in a skillet over medium heat. Add the asparagus and mushrooms and cook, stirring frequently, for 5 minutes, or until softened. Remove from the skillet and drain if necessary. Keep warm.

Meanwhile, beat the eggs with the cream, adding salt and pepper to taste.

Melt the remaining butter in a nonstick pan over medium heat. Pour in the egg mixture and cook, stirring gently with a wooden spoon, for 5–6 minutes, or until lightly set.

Arrange the ham on serving plates and top with the asparagus and mushrooms, then the egg mixture. Sprinkle with the chives and serve immediately.

SERVES 4

ingredients

4 tbsp unsalted butter

4 oz/115 g fresh baby asparagus
   spears, sliced diagonally

3 oz/85 g white mushrooms, sliced

4 eggs

3 tbsp light cream

4 thick slices lean ham

salt and pepper

1–2 tbsp snipped fresh chives,
   to garnish

Chapter Two
Main Courses

Chicken with Smoked Ham and Parmesan

30 minutes to the table

SERVES 4

ingredients

4 skinless, boneless chicken breasts
2 tbsp all-purpose flour
4 tbsp unsalted butter
8 thin slices smoked ham, trimmed
generous ½ cup freshly grated
   Parmesan cheese
salt and pepper
sprigs of fresh basil, to garnish
   (optional)

method

Cut each chicken breast through the thickness of the flesh and open out to become two separate pieces. Put the pieces between 2 sheets of plastic wrap and pound with the flat end of a meat mallet or the side of a rolling pin until the chicken is as thin as possible. Spread the flour out on a shallow plate and season to taste with salt and pepper. Coat the chicken pieces in the seasoned flour, shaking off any excess.

Melt half the butter in a large, heavy-bottom skillet over medium heat. Add the chicken pieces and cook, turning frequently, for 10-15 minutes, or until golden brown all over and cooked through.

Meanwhile, melt the remaining butter in a small pan. Remove the skillet containing the chicken from the heat. Put a slice of ham on each piece of chicken and sprinkle with the Parmesan cheese. Drizzle the melted butter over the dressed chicken, then return the skillet to the heat and cook for 3-4 minutes, or until the cheese has melted. Serve immediately, garnished with basil sprigs, if desired.

variation

Instead of the chicken breasts being cut and opened out, they can be slit to make a pocket and then filled with slices of smoked ham or prosciutto and fontina cheese before cooking.

Pepper Steak
20 minutes to the table

SERVES 4

ingredients

2 tbsp black or mixed dried
   peppercorns, coarsely crushed
4 tenderloin steaks, about 1 inch/
   2.5 cm thick, brought to room
   temperature (covered with
   plastic wrap)
1 tbsp butter
1 tsp sunflower-seed or corn oil
4 tbsp brandy
4 tbsp sour cream or heavy cream
   (optional)
salt and pepper
watercress leaves, to garnish
French fries, to serve

method

Spread the crushed peppercorns out on a plate (removing the dust) and press the steaks into them to coat on both sides.

Melt the butter with the oil in a large skillet over medium-high heat. Add the steaks in a single layer and cook for 3 minutes on each side for rare; 3½ minutes on each side for medium-rare; 4 minutes on each side for medium; and 4½–5 minutes on each side for well done.

Transfer the steaks to a warmed plate and set aside, covering with foil to keep warm. Pour the brandy into the skillet, then increase the heat and use a wooden spoon to scrape any sediment from the bottom of the skillet. Continue boiling until reduced to around 2 tablespoons.

Stir in any accumulated juices from the steaks. Spoon in the cream, if using, and continue boiling until the sauce is reduced by half again. Taste and adjust the seasoning, if necessary. Spoon the sauce over the steaks, then garnish with watercress. Serve immediately with French fries.

cook's tip

To crush the peppercorns coarsely, put them in a thick plastic bag and crush with the side of a rolling pin, removing any fine dust. Alternatively, use a pestle and mortar, but take care not to grind them too finely.

Steak in Orange Sauce
15 minutes to the table

method

Using a zester, pare a few strips of orange zest from 1 orange and reserve for the garnish. Cut the oranges in half, then cut off 4 thin slices and reserve for the garnish. Squeeze the juice from the remaining halves and set aside.

Melt the butter in a heavy-bottomed skillet over medium heat. Add the steaks and cook for 1–2 minutes on each side, or until browned and seared. Transfer the steaks to a warmed plate, and season to taste with salt and pepper. Set aside, covering with foil to keep warm.

Pour the orange juice into the skillet and add the stock and balsamic vinegar. Simmer over low heat for 2 minutes. Season the orange sauce to taste with salt and pepper and return the steaks to the skillet. Heat through gently for 2 minutes, or according to taste. Transfer to warmed serving plates and garnish with the orange slices, orange zest, and parsley leaves. Serve immediately.

cook's tip

Balsamic vinegar, from Modena in Italy, is considered to be the world's oldest and finest vinegar. It is best used in simple dishes and in salad dressings, and is available from most large supermarkets.

variation

Substitute 1 tablespoon Cointreau for 1 tablespoon of the juice squeezed from the oranges at the beginning of the method.

SERVES 4

ingredients

2 large oranges
2 tbsp butter
4 tenderloin steaks, about 6 oz/175 g each, at room temperature
6 tbsp beef stock
1 tbsp balsamic vinegar
salt and pepper
fresh flat-leaf parsley leaves, to garnish

Pork Cutlets with Fennel

30 minutes to the table

SERVES 4

ingredients

1 lb/450 g pork cutlets

2-3 tbsp extra-virgin olive oil

2 tbsp Sambuca

1 large fennel bulb, sliced, fronds reserved for garnish

generous ¾ cup crumbled Gorgonzola cheese

2 tbsp light cream

1 tbsp chopped fresh sage

1 tbsp chopped fresh thyme

salt and pepper

method

Trim any visible fat from the pork and cut into ¼-inch/5-mm thick slices. Put the slices between 2 sheets of plastic wrap and pound gently with the flat end of a meat mallet or the side of a rolling pin, until flattened slightly.

Heat 2 tablespoons of the oil in a heavy-bottomed skillet over medium heat. Add the pork, in batches, and cook for 2-3 minutes on each side, or until cooked through and tender. Transfer to a warmed plate and keep warm while you cook the remaining pork, adding more oil to the skillet, if necessary.

Pour the Sambuca into the skillet, then increase the heat and use a wooden spoon to scrape up any sediment from the bottom of the skillet. Add the fennel and cook, stirring and turning frequently, for 3 minutes. Remove the fennel from the pan and keep warm.

Reduce the heat, then add the Gorgonzola cheese and cream. Cook, stirring constantly, until smooth. Remove from the heat, then stir in the sage and thyme, and season to taste with salt and pepper.

Divide the pork and fennel between 4 warmed individual serving plates and pour over the sauce. Garnish with the reserved fennel fronds and serve immediately.

Mussels in White Wine
30 minutes to the table

SERVES 4

ingredients

4 shallots, finely chopped

3 garlic cloves, crushed

2 tbsp butter

1¼ cups dry white wine

1 bouquet garni

4 lb 8 oz/2 kg live mussels, scrubbed
   and debearded

salt and pepper

2 tbsp chopped fresh parsley,
   to garnish

method

Using a sharp knife, finely chop the shallots, then crush the garlic. Set aside. Discard any mussels with broken shells or any that refuse to close when tapped sharply.

Melt the butter in a large pot over low heat. Add the shallots and garlic and cook, stirring frequently, for 5 minutes, or until the shallots are softened. Pour in the wine, then add the bouquet garni and season to taste with salt and pepper. Bring to a boil over medium heat and add the mussels. Cover and cook, shaking the pot frequently, for 3-4 minutes, or until the mussels have opened. Discard any mussels that remain closed.

Remove and discard the bouquet garni. Using a slotted spoon, divide the mussels between 4 soup bowls. Tilt the pot and spoon a little of the cooking liquid over each plate. Sprinkle with the parsley and serve immediately.

variation

For Moules Marinière Normandy-style, substitute a good-quality dry hard cider for the wine. Replace the bouquet garni with sprigs of thyme and a bay leaf (remove the bouquet garni and bay leaf before serving.)

Mixed Seafood Curry

30 minutes to the table

method

Heat the oil in a preheated wok or large skillet over medium-high heat. Add the shallots, galangal, and garlic and stir-fry for 1-2 minutes, or until softened. Add the coconut milk, lemongrass, fish sauce, and chili sauce. Bring to a boil, then reduce the heat and simmer for 1-2 minutes.

Add the shrimp, squid, salmon, and tuna, and simmer for 3 minutes, or until the shrimp have turned pink and the fish is just cooked.

Discard any mussels with broken shells or any that refuse to close when tapped sharply. Add the mussels, then cover and simmer for 3 minutes, or until they have opened. Discard any mussels that remain closed.

Serve immediately, garnished with Chinese chives and accompanied with cooked rice.

SERVES 4

ingredients

1 tbsp vegetable oil or peanut oil

3 shallots, finely chopped

1-inch/2.5-cm piece fresh galangal, thinly sliced

2 garlic cloves, finely chopped

1¾ cups canned coconut milk

2 lemongrass stems, snapped in half

4 tbsp Thai fish sauce

2 tbsp chili sauce

8 oz/225 g raw jumbo shrimp, shelled and deveined

8 oz/225 g baby squid, cleaned and thickly sliced

8 oz/225 g salmon fillet, skinned and cut into chunks

6 oz/175 g tuna steak, cut into chunks

8 oz/225 g live mussels, scrubbed and debearded

fresh Chinese chives, to garnish

cooked rice, to serve

Broiled Tuna and Vegetable Kabobs

25 minutes to the table

method

If using wooden skewers, presoak them in cold water for 30 minutes to prevent them from burning.

Preheat the broiler to high. Cut the tuna into 1-inch/2.5-cm cubes. Peel the onions, leaving the root intact, and cut each onion lengthwise into 6 wedges.

Divide the tuna and vegetables evenly between 8 skewers and arrange on the broiler rack.

Mix the oregano and oil together in a small bowl. Season to taste with pepper. Lightly brush the kabobs with the oil mixture and cook under the preheated broiler, turning occasionally, for 10–15 minutes, or until evenly cooked.

Garnish with lime wedges and serve with a selection of salads and cooked couscous, new potatoes, or bread.

cook's tip

These kabobs can also be cooked on a grill.

SERVES 4

ingredients

4 tuna steaks, about 5 oz/140 g each
2 red onions
12 cherry tomatoes
1 red bell pepper, seeded and cut
    into 1-inch/2.5-cm pieces
1 yellow bell pepper, seeded and cut
    into 1-inch/2.5-cm pieces
1 zucchini, sliced
1 tbsp chopped fresh oregano
4 tbsp olive oil
pepper
lime wedges, to garnish

TO SERVE
selection of salads
cooked couscous, new potatoes,
    or bread

Fettuccine with Ricotta
15 minutes to the table

method

Bring a large, heavy-bottomed pan of lightly salted water to a boil. Add the pasta, then return to a boil and cook for 8-10 minutes, or until tender but still firm to the bite. Drain well and return to the pan. Add the butter and chopped parsley, reserving a few leaves for a garnish, and toss thoroughly to coat.

Mix the ricotta cheese, ground almonds, and sour cream together in a bowl. Gradually stir in the oil, followed by the hot chicken stock. Add the nutmeg and season to taste with pepper.

Transfer the pasta to a warmed serving dish, then pour over the sauce and toss to mix. Sprinkle with the pine nuts and garnish with chopped parsley leaves, then serve immediately.

cook's tip

It is important that you mix the ricotta, ground almonds, and sour cream into a smooth paste before adding the oil to the sauce. Equally, don't add the stock until the oil has been completely absorbed.

variation

To give a sharp, piquant flavor to the sauce, mix the finely grated zest and juice of ½ lemon with the ricotta cheese, ground almonds, and sour cream.

SERVES 4

ingredients

12 oz/350 g dried fettuccine

3 tbsp unsalted butter

2 tbsp chopped fresh
    flat-leaf parsley

½ cup ricotta cheese

1 cup ground almonds

⅔ cup sour cream

2 tbsp extra-virgin olive oil

½ cup hot chicken stock

pinch of freshly grated nutmeg

salt and pepper

TO GARNISH

1 tbsp pine nuts

a few leaves of chopped fresh
    flat-leaf parsley

Cauliflower and Cheese Casserole

30 minutes to the table

SERVES 4

ingredients

1 head cauliflower, about 1 lb 8 oz/
    675 g prepared weight, trimmed
    and broken into florets
1 tbsp olive oil
1 onion, thinly sliced
1 garlic clove, finely chopped
4 oz/115 g lean bacon,
    cut into ½-inch/1-cm strips
3 tbsp butter
3 tbsp all-purpose flour
generous 1¾ cups milk
generous 1 cup finely grated Cheddar
    cheese
a good grating of nutmeg
1 tbsp freshly grated Parmesan
    cheese
salt and pepper

TO SERVE
tomato salad or green salad
fresh crusty bread

method

Preheat the oven to 325°F/160°C. Put an ovenproof serving dish in the oven to warm. Cook the cauliflower in a pan of boiling salted water for 4-5 minutes—it should still be firm. Drain and transfer to the warmed serving dish, then keep warm in the oven.

Heat the oil in a skillet over medium heat. Add the onion, garlic, and bacon, and cook, stirring occasionally, for 10 minutes, or until the onion is caramelized and golden and the bacon is crisp.

Meanwhile, melt the butter in a small, heavy-bottomed pan over medium heat. Stir in the flour, until well combined and smooth. Cook, stirring constantly, for 1 minute. Remove from the heat and stir in a little of the milk, until well incorporated. Return to the heat and gradually add the remaining milk, stirring constantly. Cook, stirring, for another 3 minutes, or until the sauce is smooth and thickened. Remove from the heat and stir in the Cheddar cheese, nutmeg, and salt and pepper to taste.

Preheat the broiler to high. Spoon the onion and bacon mixture over the cauliflower and pour over the hot sauce. Sprinkle with the Parmesan cheese and cook under the preheated broiler, until browned. Serve immediately with a tomato salad or green salad, and fresh crusty bread.

Vegetable Chop Suey
15 minutes to the table

method

Heat the oil in a preheated wok or large skillet over high heat, until it is almost smoking. Add the onion and garlic and stir-fry for 30 seconds.

Add the bell peppers, broccoli, zucchini, green beans, and carrot to the wok, and stir-fry for 2-3 minutes.

Stir in the bean sprouts, sugar, soy sauce, and vegetable stock, and toss to combine thoroughly. Season to taste with salt and pepper and cook, stirring, for another 2 minutes.

Transfer the vegetables to warmed serving plates and serve immediately with cooked noodles.

cook's tip

The clever design of a wok, with its spherical bottom and high sloping sides, enables the food to be tossed so that it is cooked quickly and evenly. It is essential to heat the wok sufficiently before you add the ingredients to ensure quick and even cooking.

SERVES 4

ingredients

2 tbsp peanut oil

1 onion, chopped

3 garlic cloves, chopped

1 green bell pepper, seeded and diced

1 red bell pepper, seeded and diced

2¾ oz/75 g broccoli florets

1 zucchini, sliced

scant ¼ cup green beans

1 carrot, cut into short thin sticks

⅔ cup fresh bean sprouts

2 tsp soft light brown sugar

2 tbsp light soy sauce

½ cup vegetable stock

salt and pepper

cooked noodles, to serve

Spaghetti with Garlic and Olive Oil

15 minutes to the table

SERVES 4

ingredients

1 lb/450 g dried spaghetti

½ cup extra-virgin olive oil

3 garlic cloves, finely chopped

3 tbsp chopped fresh
   flat-leaf parsley

salt and pepper

method

Bring a large, heavy-bottomed pan of lightly salted water to a boil. Add the pasta, then return to a boil and cook for 8–10 minutes, or until tender but still firm to the bite.

Meanwhile, heat the oil in a heavy-bottomed skillet over low heat. Add the garlic and a pinch of salt and cook, stirring constantly, for 3–4 minutes, or until golden. Do not let the garlic brown, or it will taste bitter. Remove from the heat.

Drain the pasta and transfer to a warmed serving dish. Pour in the garlic-flavored oil, then add the parsley and season to taste with salt and pepper. Toss well and serve immediately.

cook's tip

Cooked pasta gets cold quickly, so make sure that the serving dish is warmed thoroughly. As soon as the pasta is drained, transfer to the dish. Pour over the garlic-flavored oil and toss, then serve.

Chapter Three
Accompaniments and Light Meals

Garlic Bread
25 minutes to the table

SERVES 4-6

ingredients

1 baguette

½ cup butter, softened

6-8 garlic cloves, finely chopped

2 tsp finely grated lemon zest
(optional)

2 tbsp chopped fresh herbs, such
as parsley, thyme, or chives, or
a mixture

method

Preheat the oven to 400°F/200°C. Slice the baguette diagonally without cutting all the way through.

Beat the butter in a bowl until creamy, then beat in the garlic, lemon zest, if using, and herbs. Alternatively, melt the butter in a small pan, then stir in the remaining ingredients.

Spread or brush the butter onto both sides of the bread slices. Put the baguette on a large sheet of foil. If there is any butter mixture remaining, dot or pour it over the top of the loaf. Bring up the long sides of the foil and fold together to enclose the loaf. Transfer to a cookie sheet and bake in the preheated oven for 15 minutes. Unwrap, then cut into separate slices and serve immediately.

Sautéed Potatoes
30 minutes to the table

method

Bring a large pan of salted water to a boil over high heat. Add the potatoes and, as soon as the water returns to a boil, drain well, then pat the potatoes completely dry with paper towels.

Melt the clarified butter (ghee) in a large sauté pan or skillet with a tight-fitting lid over medium-high heat. You want only a thin layer of butter, about ⅛ inch/3 mm deep, so, depending on the size of the pan, pour off and reserve any excess.

Add the potatoes and cook, turning frequently, for 4 minutes, or until golden all over. Add a little of the reserved clarified butter, if necessary.

Reduce the heat to very low, then cover and cook, shaking the pan occasionally, for 15–20 minutes, or until the potatoes are golden brown and offering no resistance when pierced with a knife. Add salt and pepper to taste, then stir in the parsley.

cook's tip

Cooking potatoes in butter gives them a rich flavor, but ordinary butter would probably burn before it becomes hot enough to crisp them up, which is why clarified butter, or ghee, is specified, because it can be heated to a higher temperature without burning. To make clarified butter, melt unsalted butter in a small, heavy-bottomed pan over low heat, until foaming. Skim off the foam from the surface, then drain off the clear (clarified) butter, leaving the milky residue behind. Alternatively, use 3 tablespoons unsalted butter with 1 tablespoon sunflower-seed or corn oil.

SERVES 4-6

ingredients

900 g/2 lb waxy potatoes, such as
    Charlotte, peeled and cut
    into chunks
4 tbsp clarified butter
    (see cook's tip)
salt and pepper
chopped fresh flat-leaf parsley or
    scallions, to garnish

Warm Potatoes with Pesto

25 minutes to the table

method

Cook the potatoes in a large pan of salted boiling water for
15 minutes, or until tender. Drain, then transfer to a salad bowl and
let cool slightly.

Add the pesto sauce to the potatoes, and salt and pepper to taste,
and toss thoroughly to coat. Sprinkle with the Parmesan cheese and
serve immediately.

cook's tip

Pesto sauce, originally from Genoa in Italy, is made with fresh basil,
pine nuts, garlic, Parmesan cheese, and olive oil. You can buy good-
quality, fresh pesto in supermarkets.

SERVES 4

ingredients

1 lb/450 g small new potatoes

3 tsp pesto sauce

¼ cup freshly grated Parmesan
cheese

salt and pepper

Asparagus with Melted Butter

10 minutes to the table

method

Bring a medium pan of salted water to a boil. Meanwhile, remove some of the bottom of the thicker asparagus stalks with a potato peeler. Tie the stems together with clean string or use a wire basket so that they can easily be removed from the pan without damage.

Plunge the stems into the boiling water, then cover and cook for 4-5 minutes. Pierce a stem near the bottom with a sharp knife. If fairly soft, remove the pan from the heat immediately. Do not overcook asparagus, or the tender tips will fall off.

Drain the asparagus thoroughly and serve on large, warmed plates with the melted butter poured over. Both the butter and the asparagus should be warm rather than hot. Serve with the salt and pepper, and hand out large napkins!

variations

To broil asparagus, brush a broiler pan with oil and then heat, until it is very hot. Add the asparagus and cook for 2 minutes on one side, then turn over and cook for another 2 minutes. Serve immediately. Asparagus is also delicious served with slices of prosciutto, fresh shavings of Parmesan cheese, or soft-cooked quail's eggs. Alternatively, cook 1 cup fresh white bread crumbs in 3 tablespoons butter, until golden and crisp, and serve scattered over lightly cooked asparagus.

SERVES 2

ingredients

16-20 fresh asparagus spears, trimmed to about 8 inches/20 cm in length

generous 6 tbsp unsalted butter, melted

sea salt and pepper

Warm Pasta Salad
20 minutes to the table

SERVES 4

ingredients

8 oz/225 g dried farfalle or other
    pasta shapes
6 pieces sun-dried tomato in oil,
    drained and chopped
4 scallions, chopped
2 oz/55 g arugula, shredded
½ cucumber, seeded and diced
2 tbsp freshly grated Parmesan
    cheese
salt and pepper

DRESSING
4 tbsp olive oil
½ tsp superfine sugar
1 tbsp white wine vinegar
1 tsp Dijon mustard
4 fresh basil leaves,
    finely shredded
salt and pepper

method

Bring a large, heavy-bottomed pan of lightly salted water to a boil. Add the pasta, then return to a boil and cook for 8–10 minutes, or until tender but still firm to the bite.

Meanwhile, to make the dressing, whisk the oil, sugar, vinegar, and mustard together in a bowl. Season to taste with salt and pepper. Stir in the basil.

Drain the pasta and transfer to a salad bowl. Add the dressing and toss thoroughly to coat.

Add the sun-dried tomatoes, scallions, arugula, and cucumber. Season to taste with salt and pepper, then toss well. Sprinkle with the Parmesan cheese and serve warm.

cook's tip

It is easier to toss the pasta if you use 2 forks or 2 tablespoons, and before adding the dressing to the salad, whisk it again, until emulsified. Add the dressing just before serving.

Salade Niçoise
30 minutes to the table

SERVES 4-8

ingredients

2 tuna steaks, about ¾ inch/
   2 cm thick
olive oil, for brushing
1⅔ cups green beans
2 lettuce hearts, leaves separated
3 large hard-cooked eggs,
   cut into fourths
2 juicy vine-ripened tomatoes,
   cut into wedges
1¾ oz/50 g anchovy fillets in oil,
   drained
⅓ cup Niçoise olives
salt and pepper
fresh basil leaves, torn, to garnish
French bread, to serve

DRESSING
½ cup extra-virgin olive oil
3 tbsp white wine vinegar or lemon
   juice
1-2 garlic cloves, crushed, to taste
1 tsp Dijon mustard
½ tsp superfine sugar

method

Heat a ridged, cast-iron grill pan over high heat, until you can feel the heat rising from the surface. Brush the tuna steaks with oil, then add, oiled-side down, to the grill pan, and cook for 2 minutes.

Lightly brush the top side of the tuna steaks with a little more oil. Use a pair of tongs to turn the tuna steaks over, then season to taste with salt and pepper. Cook for another 2 minutes for rare or up to 4 minutes for well done. Let cool.

Meanwhile, bring a pan of salted water to a boil. Add the beans, then return to a boil and cook for 3 minutes, or until tender-crisp. Drain and immediately transfer to a large bowl. Put all the ingredients for the dressing in a screw-top jar, then screw on the lid and shake vigorously, until an emulsion forms. Pour the dressing over the beans and stir together. Let the beans cool in the dressing.

To serve, line a platter with lettuce leaves. Lift the beans out of the bowl, leaving the excess dressing behind, and pile in the center of the platter. Break the tuna into large flakes and arrange over the beans.

Arrange the hard-cooked eggs and the tomatoes around the side and the anchovy fillets over the salad, then add the olives and basil. Drizzle the remaining dressing in the bowl over everything and serve with plenty of French bread for mopping up the dressing.

Caesar Salad
15 minutes to the table

SERVES 4

ingredients

1 large egg

2 romaine lettuces or 3 Boston
   lettuces, leaves separated

6 tbsp olive oil

2 tbsp lemon juice

8 canned anchovy fillets, drained
   and coarsely chopped

generous ¾ cup fresh Parmesan
   cheese shavings

salt and pepper

GARLIC CROUTONS

4 tbsp olive oil

2 garlic cloves, finely chopped

5 slices white bread, crusts removed,
   cut into ½-inch/1-cm cubes

method

Bring a small, heavy-bottomed pan of water to a boil.

Meanwhile, to make the croutons, heat the oil in a heavy-bottomed skillet over medium-high heat. Add the garlic and bread cubes and cook, stirring and tossing frequently, for 4–5 minutes, or until the bread is crisp and golden all over. Remove with a slotted spoon and drain on paper towels.

While the bread is cooking, add the egg to the boiling water and cook for 1 minute, then remove and set aside.

Arrange the lettuce leaves in a salad bowl. Mix the oil and lemon juice together in a bowl, then season to taste with salt and pepper. Crack the egg into the dressing and whisk thoroughly until blended. Pour the dressing over the lettuce leaves, toss well, then add the croutons and anchovies and toss the salad again. Sprinkle with the Parmesan cheese shavings and serve.

cook's tip

Don't let the salad stand around too long after the dressing has been added, or the lettuce will go soggy and the salad will be unusable.

caution

Recipes using very lightly cooked eggs should be avoided by infants, the elderly, pregnant women, convalescents, and anyone suffering from an illness.

Mixed Seafood Salad
20 minutes to the table

method

Discard any mussels with broken shells or any that refuse to close when tapped. Heat 1 tablespoon of oil in a preheated wok or large skillet over high heat. Add the onion, squid, shrimp, and mussels, and stir-fry for 2 minutes, or until the squid is opaque and the mussels have opened. Discard any mussels that remain closed.

Meanwhile, mix the scallions, lemongrass, red bell pepper, and napa cabbage together in a bowl. Add the seafood and stir gently together. Turn into a serving dish.

For the dressing, mix the garlic, 2 tablespoons of oil, the fish sauce, jaggery, and lemon juice together in a small bowl. Stir in the cucumber and tomato, then spoon the dressing over the salad and seafood, and serve immediately.

SERVES 4

ingredients

1 lb 2 oz/500 g live mussels, scrubbed and debearded
1 tbsp vegetable oil or peanut oil
1 small onion, thinly sliced
8 oz/225 g baby squid, cleaned and sliced
8 oz/225 g cooked shrimp, shelled and deveined
bunch of scallions, coarsely chopped
1 lemongrass stem, outer leaves removed, finely chopped
1 red bell pepper, seeded and cut into strips
½ small head napa cabbage, shredded

DRESSING
2 garlic cloves, crushed
2 tbsp vegetable oil or peanut oil
1 tsp Thai fish sauce
1 tsp jaggery or soft light brown sugar
juice of 1 lemon
2-inch/5-cm piece cucumber, chopped
1 tomato, seeded and chopped

Walnut, Pear, and Crispy Bacon Salad

25 minutes to the table

method

Preheat the broiler to high. Arrange the bacon on a broiler rack and cook under the preheated broiler, or until well browned and crisp. Let cool, then cut into ½-inch/1-cm pieces.

Meanwhile, heat a dry skillet over medium heat. Add the walnuts and dry-fry, shaking the skillet frequently, for 3 minutes, or until lightly browned. Remove from the skillet and let cool.

Toss the pears in the lemon juice to prevent discoloration. Transfer the watercress, walnuts, pears, and bacon to a salad bowl.

To make the dressing, whisk the oil, lemon juice, and honey together in a small bowl or pitcher. Season to taste with salt and pepper, then pour over the salad. Toss well to combine and serve immediately.

SERVES 4

ingredients

4 lean Canadian bacon strips

scant ¾ cup walnut halves

2 Red William pears, cored and sliced lengthwise

1 tbsp lemon juice

6 oz/175 g watercress, tough stems removed

DRESSING

3 tbsp extra-virgin olive oil

2 tbsp lemon juice

½ tsp clear honey

salt and pepper

Chapter Four
Desserts

Strawberry Baked Alaska

20 minutes to the table

SERVES 6

ingredients

9-inch/23-cm round sponge cake

2 tbsp sweet sherry or orange juice

5 egg whites

¾ cup superfine sugar

2 cups strawberry ice cream

scant 1 cup fresh strawberries, hulled
   and halved, plus whole
   strawberries, to serve

method

Preheat the oven to 475°F/240°C. Put the sponge cake in a large, shallow, ovenproof pan and sprinkle with the sherry.

Whisk the egg whites in a spotlessly clean, grease-free bowl, until stiff. Continue to whisk, gradually adding the sugar, until very stiff and glossy.

Working quickly, cover the top of the cake with the ice cream and then top with the strawberry halves. Spread the meringue mixture over the cake, making sure that the ice cream is completely covered. Bake in the preheated oven for 3–5 minutes, or until the meringue is golden brown. Serve immediately, with whole strawberries.

cook's tip

For the perfect meringue, bring the egg whites to room temperature before whisking. It is worth noting that the fresher the eggs, the greater the volume of the meringue.

Chocolate Fondue
15 minutes to the table

SERVES 4

ingredients
8 squares semisweet chocolate
generous ¾ cup heavy cream
2 tbsp brandy

TO SERVE
selection of prepared fresh fruit
white and pink marshmallows
sweet cookies

method
Break the chocolate into small pieces and put in a small pan with the cream. Heat the mixture over low heat, stirring constantly, until the chocolate has melted and blended with the cream.

Remove from the heat and stir in the brandy.

Pour the mixture into a fondue pot or small, flameproof dish and keep warm over a small burner.

Serve with a selection of prepared fresh fruit (see cook's tip), marshmallows, and cookies for dipping. The fruit and marshmallows can be spiked on fondue forks, wooden skewers, or ordinary forks for dipping into the chocolate fondue.

cook's tip
To prepare the fruit for dipping, cut larger fruit into bite-size pieces. Fruit that discolors, such as bananas, apples, and pears, should be dipped in a little lemon juice as soon as they are cut.

variation
Choose your favorite fruit to dip in the fondue. Kiwifruit, banana chunks, apple pieces, and strawberries go particularly well.

Broiled Peaches and Sour Cream

15 minutes to the table

method

Preheat the broiler to medium. Plunge the peaches in a pan of boiling water for 1 minute. Remove and refresh under cold running water, then peel, halve, pit, and slice. Arrange the peach slices in 4 individual flameproof dishes.

Mix the brown sugar and cinnamon together and sprinkle the mixture over the peaches. Spoon the sour cream on top, then sprinkle 1 tablespoon of superfine sugar over each dish.

Cook under the preheated broiler for 2–3 minutes, or until the superfine sugar has melted and caramelized. Serve immediately or let cool.

cook's tip

To pit peaches, cut vertically around the fruit, then twist each half in opposite directions to reveal the pit. Using the point of a knife, prise the pit out and remove with your fingers, then discard.

SERVES 4

ingredients

4 large, fresh, ripe peaches
2 tbsp soft light brown sugar
½ tsp ground cinnamon
1¼ cups sour cream
4 tbsp superfine sugar

Semolina Dessert
20 minutes to the table

SERVES 4

ingredients

6 tbsp vegetable oil or peanut oil

3 cloves

3 green cardamom pods

8 tbsp coarse semolina

½ tsp ground saffron

⅓ cup golden raisins

⅔ cup superfine sugar

1¼ cups water

1¼ cups milk

light cream, to serve

TO DECORATE

⅓ cup dry unsweetened coconut,
    toasted

scant ¼ cup chopped almonds

scant ¼ cup skinned, chopped
    pistachios (optional)

method

Melt the oil in a pan over medium heat.

   Add the cloves and cardamom pods to the melted butter, then reduce the heat and stir to mix.

   Add the semolina and cook, until it turns a little darker.

   Add the saffron, golden raisins, and sugar to the semolina mixture, stirring to mix well.

   Pour in the water and milk and bring to a boil, stirring. Reduce the heat and simmer, stirring constantly, for 10 minutes, or until the semolina is cooked. Add a little more water if necessary.

   Remove from the heat and transfer the semolina to a warmed serving dish.

   Decorate with the toasted coconut and almonds, and pistachios if using. Serve with a little cream drizzled over the top.

Exotic Fruit Cocktail
20 minutes to the table

SERVES 4

ingredients

2 oranges
2 large passion fruit
1 pineapple
1 pomegranate
1 banana

method

Cut 1 orange in half and squeeze the juice into a bowl, discarding any seeds. Using a sharp knife, cut away all the peel and pith from the second orange. Working over the bowl to catch the juice, carefully cut the orange segments between the membranes to obtain skinless segments of fruit. Discard any seeds.

Cut the passion fruit in half. Scoop the flesh into a nylon strainer, and, using a spoon, push the pulp and juice into the bowl of orange segments. Discard the seeds.

Using a sharp knife, cut away all the skin from the pineapple and cut the flesh lengthwise into fourths. Cut away the central hard core. Cut the flesh into chunks and add to the orange and passion fruit mixture. Cover with plastic wrap and refrigerate the fruit at this stage if you are not serving the fruit cocktail immediately.

Cut the pomegranate into quarters and, using your fingers or a teaspoon, remove the red seeds from the membrane. Cover and refrigerate until ready to serve—do not add too early to the fruit cocktail because the seeds will discolor the other fruit.

Just before serving, peel and slice the banana. Add to the fruit cocktail with the pomegranate seeds, and mix thoroughly. Serve the fruit cocktail immediately.

Banana-Stuffed Crêpes

25 minutes to the table

method

Sift the flour into a bowl and stir in the sugar. Make a well in the center. Add the eggs and milk to the well and gradually beat into the flour mixture to form a smooth batter. Stir in the lemon zest.

Melt a little butter in an 8-inch/20-cm skillet over medium-high heat and pour in a quarter of the batter. Tilt the skillet to coat the bottom and cook for 1–2 minutes, or until the underside is set. Flip the crêpe over and cook the other side for 1 minute. Slide it out of the skillet and keep warm. Repeat to make 3 more crêpes.

Slice the bananas and toss in the lemon juice in a bowl. Pour over the syrup and toss together. Fold each crêpe into 4 and fill the center with the banana mixture. Serve warm.

SERVES 4

ingredients

generous 1½ cups all-purpose flour
2 tbsp soft light brown sugar
2 eggs
scant 2 cups milk
grated zest of 1 lemon
4 tbsp butter

FILLING
3 bananas
juice of 1 lemon
4 tbsp corn syrup

Fruit Kabobs
20 minutes to the table

method
Select skewers that will fit comfortably in your broiler pan. If using wooden skewers, presoak them in cold water for 30 minutes to prevent them from burning.

Preheat the broiler pan over medium heat.

Pit the fruit as necessary, or remove cores, and cut into similar-size pieces. Small fruit may be left whole. Arrange alternating pieces on the skewers. Brush the fruit with the melted butter.

Spread the sugar out on a plate large enough to take the skewers. Mix in the cinnamon, if using. Roll the fruit kabobs in the sugar, pressing gently to coat.

Add the kabobs to the broiler pan and cook, turning occasionally, for 10 minutes, or until the sugar has melted and started to bubble. The fruit should still be firm.

Serve immediately, with heavy cream, strained plain yogurt, or ice cream.

SERVES 4

ingredients
1 lb/450 g assorted fresh fruit, such
   as peaches, apricots, plums, apples,
   and pears
4 tbsp butter, melted
2 tbsp sugar
pinch of ground cinnamon (optional)

SERVING SUGGESTIONS
heavy cream
strained plain yogurt
ice cream

Foaming Froth
20 minutes to the table

SERVES 4

ingredients

4 egg yolks
5 tbsp superfine sugar
5 tbsp Marsala wine
amaretti cookies, to serve

method

Whisk the egg yolks with the sugar in a heatproof bowl or, if you have one, in the top of a double boiler for about 1 minute.

Gently whisk in the Marsala. Set the bowl over a pan of barely simmering water, or put the top of the double boiler on its bottom filled with barely simmering water, and whisk vigorously for 10–15 minutes, or until thick, creamy, and foamy.

Immediately pour the drink into serving glasses and serve with amaretti cookies.

variations

You can use other wines, such as Champagne, Sauternes, or Madeira, to flavor this dessert, or a liqueur, such as Chartreuse or Cointreau. Or try mixing white wine with brandy, rum, or Maraschino.

caution

Recipes using very lightly cooked eggs should be avoided by infants, the elderly, pregnant women, convalescents, and anyone suffering from an illness.

Cherry Crêpes
25 minutes to the table

method

Drain the cherries, reserving 1¼ cups of the can juice. Put the cherries and juice in a pan with the almond extract and allspice. Stir in the cornstarch, until well incorporated. Bring to a boil and cook, stirring constantly, until thickened and clear. Remove from the heat and set aside.

To make the crêpes, sift the flour and salt into a bowl. Stir in the mint. Make a well in the center. Add the egg and milk to the well and gradually beat into the flour to form a smooth batter.

Heat 1 tablespoon of oil in a 7-inch/18-cm skillet over medium-high heat, and pour off the oil when hot. Pour in a quarter of the batter. Tilt the skillet to coat the bottom and cook for 1–2 minutes, until the underside is set. Flip the crêpe over and cook the other side for 1 minute. Slide it out of the skillet and keep warm. Repeat to make 3 more crêpes.

Spoon a quarter of the cherry mixture onto a quarter of each crêpe and fold the crêpe into a cone shape. Dust with confectioners' sugar and sprinkle toasted slivered almonds over the top. Serve immediately.

SERVES 4

ingredients

14 oz/400 g canned pitted cherries
½ tsp almond extract
½ tsp ground allspice
2 tbsp cornstarch

CREPES
generous ⅔ cup all-purpose flour
pinch of salt
2 tbsp chopped fresh mint
1 egg
1¼ cups milk
vegetable oil, for cooking

TO DECORATE
confectioners' sugar
toasted slivered almonds

Index